CW01512855

Original title:
Inky Snow Among the Griffin Dell

Author: Johan Kirsipuu
ISBN HARDBACK: 978-1-80563-251-1
ISBN PAPERBACK: 978-1-80564-772-0

Secrets Hidden Under a Blanket of White

In a whisper of snow, the world turns so still,
Soft shadows are dancing, where winter winds chill.
Beneath the bright surface, the secrets confide,
A tapestry woven where silence will bide.

The moon casts a glow on the paths yet untread,
While dreams take their flight on the wings of the dead.
In pockets of twilight, old tales intertwine,
As echoes of magic in frostbound lines shine.

Invisible wonders, where lost spirits roam,
Nestle in silence, seeking solace and home.
Each flake tells a story, forgotten yet dear,
Whispers of ages held close, ever near.

The pines wear their coats, heavy, soft, and white,
Guarding the secrets that slumber at night.
They rustle with laughter, with secrets that gleam,
Awakening shadows in a magical dream.

So pause for a moment beneath starlit skies,
For hidden amidst the stillness, truth lies.
The snow may be white, but beneath it all glows,
A world of enchantment, where wonder still grows.

Dark Feathers Adrift on Winter's Breath

In twilight realms where shadows play,
Black feathers drift on winter's sway.
They whisper tales of dreams unspun,
Beneath the rays of a pale, lost sun.

The chill winds weave a haunting song,
Echoes of sorrow, where hearts belong.
Each feather dances with secrets cold,
Telling stories of the bold and the old.

In silent sighs, the night unfolds,
A tapestry of memories, woven in folds.
With every gust that stirs the night,
Hope and despair take flight in white.

Yet in the shadows, glimmers of light,
Faint as the stars, they guide the night.
For in the dark, where feathers roam,
Lies the promise of journeys home.

The Haunting of the Frost-Kissed Forest

The forest sleeps, wrapped in frost,
Whispers of warmth in echoes lost.
Beneath the branches, pale and bare,
Spirits linger, hidden with care.

Silver dew on every leaf,
A testament to winter's grief.
Lost laughter lingers in the air,
For tales untold through silence share.

With every step, the shadows creep,
Awakening secrets the trees do keep.
Frost-kissed stones where dreams have bled,
In every corner, the echoes spread.

A haunting melody softly sings,
Of ancient magic and winter's wings.
As moonlight bathes the frozen ground,
Embers of stories lost are found.

Nocturnal Secrets Beneath the Moonlight

Beneath the moon, a world unfolds,
Where twilight's magic gently holds.
Nocturnal whispers fill the night,
Tales of wonder, hidden from sight.

The owls observe with knowing eyes,
Guardians of secrets, beneath the skies.
Each rustle of leaves, each sigh of breeze,
Weaves a spell that aims to please.

Stars twinkle like diamonds bright,
Guiding those who fancy flight.
In shadows deep, the truth is sown,
In the moon's glow, dreams are grown.

A lullaby for the dreaming hearts,
Where reality ends and magic starts.
For beneath the moon's soft embrace,
All wanderers find their sacred place.

The Grimoire of Frost and Feather

In a tome of frost adorned with plume,
Secrets stir in the winter's gloom.
Pages whisper of spells long past,
Echoes of magic that forever last.

Each feather inked with stories unknown,
In the grimoire's heart, the truth has grown.
Chants of power draped in icy threads,
Awakening dreams from their frozen beds.

The flicker of firelight dances bright,
Illuminating paths in the shrouded night.
With every turn, the courage speaks,
In shadows where the ancient seeks.

Through winter's breath and midnight's veil,
The legacy of feathered tales prevail.
For those who dare to seek and see,
The grimoire's secrets set them free.

Twilight's Ink over a Pale World

In the hush of eve, shadows grow,
Whispering secrets through twilight's glow.
Stars like distant gems start to gleam,
Painting the world in a silver dream.

Ghostly whispers tease the night,
As owls take flight in search of light.
The moon stretches wide, a guardian's eye,
Watching the dreams of the world drift by.

Beneath the ink, soft visions creep,
Through valleys of silence where memories sleep.
Every heartbeat a story, old yet bold,
In twilight's embrace, our truths unfold.

Colors blend into a swirling hue,
As darkness wraps around the dew.
The lingering scents of earth and air,
Fill the dusk, a lullaby's farewell.

So let the twilight spill its ink,
Over a world on the edge of a wink.
In the palette of night, our destinies flow,
Guided by stars, where the heartbeats know.

The Guardians of the Whispering Woods

In the woods where the ancients dwell,
Gentle spirits weave their spell.
Leaves whisper tales of long-lost nights,
Under the embrace of shimmering lights.

Branch and bough, a fortress strong,
Echoing the softest song.
Moss carpets the ground, like a throne,
Where timeless guardians stand alone.

Each rustling leaf a quiet plea,
To those who wander, wild and free.
The essence of magic hangs in the air,
As secrets unfold beneath their care.

Brightness dances 'neath the canopy,
Illuminating shadows, a symphony.
Paths intertwined, destiny's call,
The guardians stand watch, over all.

Their whispers guide the weary heart,
In nature's fold, we play our part.
For in the depths of the whispering woods,
Lies the essence of life, and all things good.

Wraiths of Winter in Glistening White

In silence deep, the snowy night,
Wraiths of winter take their flight.
Veils of frost twirl in the air,
As moonlight glistens everywhere.

Branches bow with a heavy crown,
While shadows dance on the frozen down.
Footsteps muffled, a soft, cold hymn,
Echoing still, where the light grows dim.

Blankets of white cover the ground,
In the stillness, whispers resound.
The chill forges tales of ice,
Where all is tranquil, yet precise.

Wraiths weave stories under the stars,
Mapping their paths on the wayward scars.
Each breath a fog in the breath of frost,
A moment cherished, never lost.

Winter silhouettes, both bold and slight,
Guarding the dreams of the endless night.
As dawn shall break, with the sun's warm kiss,
Wraiths will fade into dream's soft bliss.

Dark Wings and Hallowed Ground

On the edge of twilight, shadows rise,
Dark wings spread under stormy skies.
Echoes of fate, they softly pound,
As night enfolds the hallowed ground.

Beneath the stars, a whisper clears,
Haunting thoughts of forgotten years.
The weight of worlds rests on their flight,
Guided by instinct, both fierce and bright.

With every beat, a tale is spun,
Legacies chase the wandering sun.
In the night's embrace, truths are found,
Carved in silence on the hallowed ground.

They dance with shadows, swift and bold,
Guardians of stories yet untold.
Every breath a connection profound,
Revealing secrets on the hallowed ground.

So gather close, hear the call,
Of dark wings soaring, lest we fall.
For in their shadowed hymn, we see,
A spirit's path toward eternity.

Frostbitten Tales of the Ancient Roost

In ancient woods where shadows play,
The frost-kissed boughs, a ghostly sway.
Whispers echo, secrets bound,
In every rustle, magic found.

From frosty heights, the owls do hoot,
Guardians of lore in branches rooted.
With wings like clouds, they glide, they soar,
Their tales of yore forever pour.

Beneath the stars, a silvery light,
Illuminates the creatures of night.
Frozen air, a spell so deep,
Lulls the weary wood to sleep.

Within the stillness, stories weave,
What once was lost, we dare believe.
Each frostbitten tale, a heart's refrain,
In the silent woods, love's shadow reigns.

So tread softly on the icy ground,
Where ancient spirits linger around.
In every flake, a tale untold,
Frostbitten dreams in the winter's hold.

The Specter of Nightfall in White

As daylight wanes and shadows creep,
The specter walks where secrets sleep.
Cloaked in white, with eyes aglow,
Through misty realms, she weaves her flow.

In moonlit glades, the silence sighs,
Whispers carried on the night's soft cries.
A gentle breeze, a fleeting breath,
Chasing tales of love and death.

Her dance of shadows, a haunting waltz,
In every twirl, the world exalts.
Lingering echoes of hope and despair,
The specter of nightfall, beyond compare.

While stars bear witness to her plight,
In the depths of the cold, starry night,
She wanders through dreams, both lost and found,
In barren woods, where spirits abound.

So if you wander on a winter's eve,
And feel the chill that makes you grieve,
Remember the specter, soft and slight,
In the embrace of the deepening night.

Twilight Silhouettes of the Feathered King

Beneath the glow of setting sun,
The Feathered King, a tale begun.
With wings of dusk, he takes his flight,
Through twilight hues of rich delight.

His silhouette against the blaze,
A regal form in sunset's gaze.
He sings of days both brave and bold,
Of ancient truths and legends old.

With every flap, the darkness sighs,
In spirals spun beneath the skies.
As stars appear, he guards the night,
A gentle keeper of the light.

In forests deep, where shadows play,
He dances through the breaking day.
A symbol strong, a spirit free,
The Feathered King, our destiny.

So heed his call when dusk descends,
As twilight whispers, the mystery bends.
In the drape of night, let kinship cling,
To the twilight silhouettes of the Feathered King.

Shimmering Silhouettes in the Quiet Thicket

In thickets deep where silence dwells,
A world awakens, weaving spells.
Shimmering forms in moonlight's glow,
A dance of shadows, soft and slow.

The cricket's song, a gentle cheer,
As hidden creatures draw so near.
With every rustle, secrets stir,
In the quiet thicket, hearts confer.

From emerald leaves, a glimmer bright,
Illuminates the lingering night.
Each flicker holds a tale untold,
Of magic woven in threads of gold.

As stars peek through the leafy veil,
The shimmering silhouettes unveil.
Each heartbeat in the night does sing,
Of wonder found in the thicket's spring.

So wander forth where peace resides,
In quiet thickets, let joy be your guide.
For in the stillness, life takes wing,
In shimmering silhouettes, we find our spring.

The Mysterious Vale of Winter's Call

In a vale where whispers sigh,
The frost-kissed trees stand high.
Moonlight paints the chill tonight,
As secrets dance in silver light.

Footprints lead to paths unknown,
Where ancient stories are overgrown.
The winter's breath, a ghostly song,
Calls to hearts where dreams belong.

Stars above, a twinkling map,
Guide the souls within the trap.
In stillness, magic takes its flight,
With each flutter, hearts ignite.

Echoes carry on the breeze,
Rustling leaves like whispered pleas.
Enchantments weave through twilight air,
Inviting all who wander there.

So tread lightly, brave and bold,
In the vale where stories unfold.
For winter's call, a siren's plea,
Holds the key to mystery.

Silhouettes in the Ethereal Snow

Silhouettes in moonlit glow,
Dance upon the blankets of snow.
Whispers glide on icy streams,
Where reality blends with dreams.

Figures leap with silent grace,
In this enchanted, timeless space.
Frosty breath and twinkling eyes,
Bewitching under starry skies.

Softly steps on crystal ground,
Nature's magic all around.
In the stillness, shadows play,
Guiding night till break of day.

Amidst the flakes that gently fall,
Echoes of the ancients call.
Longing hearts unite their fears,
In this world that disappears.

Each moment cherished, pure, and bright,
In ethereal, sparkling light.
Together lost, we find our way,
Through silhouettes of winter's sway.

Shadows of the Night's Majestic Creatures

Beneath the cloak of twilight's veil,
The shadows stir, the nightingale.
Majestic creatures glide with ease,
In harmony with rustling leaves.

Owl's eyes gleam like distant stars,
Guardians of the world from afar.
Through the darkness, wise and keen,
They watch the whispers in between.

Foxes dance in fleeting light,
Crafting secrets of the night.
With every pawprint left behind,
Lies a story yet to find.

Their songs are woven through the trees,
Carried gently on the breeze.
In every lark and every cry,
A tale of wonder floating by.

As moonlit beams pierce through the dark,
Each heartbeat whispers, leaves its mark.
Join the shadows, roam the wild,
Embrace the night, forever beguiled.

Secrets of the Winged Keepers

In the hush of dusky skies,
Flutters secrets that arise.
Winged keepers, bold and bright,
Guard the realms of day and night.

With feathers brushed by twilight air,
They weave their tales with utmost care.
In every flap, a whisper flows,
Of hidden paths where magic grows.

Above the world, in graceful arcs,
They sketch the sky with gentle marks.
Gliding softly through the gloom,
Guardians of the night's sweet bloom.

Each caw a message, rich and clear,
Calling those who dare draw near.
To see the wonders, bright and bold,
Of the secrets they have told.

So listen close when shadows breeze,
For winged keepers know with ease.
Their stories pulse within your heart,
A symphony that won't depart.

Frosted Wings Beneath Starlit Canopy

In the hush of winter's night,
Frosted wings take flight,
A shimmer on the snow,
Beneath stars that softly glow.

Whispers float on chilled air,
Secrets shared with the rare,
Each tick of time held dear,
In harmony, the world draws near.

Silence wraps the slumbering wood,
A magic only dreamers could,
Where shadows blend with frost,
And every care feels lost.

Breezes weave through boughs of pine,
As owls hoot in gentle rhyme,
Underneath the endless sky,
Where wishes breathe and fly.

Spirits dance in moonlit mist,
In their wonder we exist,
Frosted wings, a fleeting sight,
Claiming peace in starry light.

The Lament of the Shadowed Glade

In the heart where shadows creep,
Secrets hidden, silence deep,
Branches sigh with ancient grief,
In twilight, seeking relief.

Whispers curl around the trees,
Echoes borne on dusky breeze,
Every leaf a story told,
Of glories lost and hearts gone cold.

The moon casts dreams upon the ground,
A symphony of lost sounds,
Melodies of yesteryear,
Resonate but none can hear.

Footfalls fade in muted woods,
Where once great heroes stood,
A lament soft, like a sigh,
In the gloaming that drifts by.

Time weaves through each gnarled root,
Life returns in tender shoot,
Yet shadows linger, a gentle chase,
In the glade's embrace, we face.

Echoes of a Snowy Night's Enigma

Underneath a quilt of white,
The world holds its breath in night,
Softly falls the silver snow,
Secrets in its depths bestow.

The stars like diamonds shine so bright,
Mysteries in their gleaming light,
Each flake a whispered grace,
In this tranquil, frozen place.

Footprints mark a curious path,
Leading into winter's wrath,
But echoes chase with every breath,
In the dance of life and death.

Hushed are tales that linger here,
Fables spun in crystal clear,
Dreams are woven, soft as air,
In the magic everywhere.

In the stillness, truths unfold,
Wonders both the shy and bold,
A snowy night, a world anew,
Where enigmas drift and strew.

Where the Gryphon Soars in Silence

High above the mountain's crest,
Where the air is braced and blessed,
The gryphon calls the skies its home,
In realms where wild spirits roam.

Wings spread wide in vibrant grace,
Racing clouds in a timeless chase,
In silence, majesty takes flight,
Transforming day to velvet night.

Beneath the sun's embracing glow,
Ancient tales begin to flow,
Legends born of fierce delight,
Illuminated in purest light.

Gliding over cliffs so steep,
Guardians of dreams we keep,
With every beat, a whisper flies,
Where the heart of courage lies.

In the vastness, wild and grand,
Gryphons soar, an angel band,
Riders of the skies, so bold,
In their wings, the stories told.

The Frost-Kissed Spirit of the Woodland

In the dappled light, shadows weave,
Whispers of winter, tales believe.
Beneath the branches, secrets sigh,
Where the frost-kissed spirit flits by.

Glimmers of silver on leaf and stone,
The woodland sings, yet feels alone.
Each twinkle dances, a soft refrain,
In the heart of the woods, where dreams remain.

Hushed are the paths, where footsteps tread,
Memories linger, softly spread.
Echoes of laughter, long since passed,
In the frost-kissed boughs, peace amassed.

Crystals adorn the quiet glade,
While twilight's charm begins to fade.
A flickered glow draws the eye confined,
In the sacred woods, serenity aligned.

The spirit dwells where silence breathes,
Nature's cradle, a tapestry weaves.
Frost envelops the ancient tree,
In this enchanted realm, wild and free.

A Winter's Song Understarred and Dark

In the stillness of night, stars abound,
Winter's song whispers, soft and profound.
Under the blanket of velvet skies,
The moonlight glistens, magic implies.

Frosted branches sway in the breeze,
Crystals dance lightly, as if to please.
An owl calls out, wise and forlorn,
In the heart of the night, new dreams are born.

Footsteps crunch on the crisp, white snow,
Echoes of secrets begin to grow.
A melody weaves through shadows deep,
Woven with wonders, a lullaby to keep.

Beneath the vastness, a shimmer glows,
Each star a promise, the night bestows.
In the depth of winter, hope shines bright,
Guiding lost souls through the darkened night.

So let the world listen, hearts entwined,
To the winter's song where magic's signed.
Through the cold and the silence, love shall spark,
In this hush of winter, understarred and dark.

Veils of Winter in the Enchanted Forest

Veils of winter cloak the trees,
Whispers of magic carried by the breeze.
Each flake that falls, a tale unfolds,
In the enchanted forest, mysteries told.

Glistening paths where shadows play,
Crimson berries burst, bright as day.
Footsteps lead to realms unknown,
Where nature's beauty stands alone.

Branches bow low with a silver crown,
A quiet blanket, the world slows down.
In a trance of wonder, silence reigns,
In this timeless dance, nothing remains.

Every glimpse through frosty air,
Reveals the enchantment beyond compare.
Where faeries hide in the moon's soft glow,
Veils of winter, a shimmering show.

In the heart of twilight, dreams take flight,
Under the stars, a wondrous sight.
So wander forth where the magic breeds,
In the veils of winter, your spirit leads.

The Frost's Embrace in the Gryphon's Nest

High on the hill, where eagles soar,
In the gryphon's nest, the chill evermore.
Frost paints feathers, glistening white,
Cuddled within warmth, hidden from sight.

The world below is wrapped in snow,
While ancient tales of valor grow.
With a watchful eye, the guardian waits,
In the frost's embrace, destiny baits.

Each morning brings a golden glow,
As sunlight dances on hills below.
A gentle caress from the sun's embrace,
Waking the secrets of this sacred space.

And when the night drapes its inky shawl,
The gryphon whispers to the stars, enthralled.
In the silence, dreams take wing,
As winter cradles, the heart will sing.

So cherish the moment, hold it tight,
In the gryphon's nest, all feels right.
For in the frost's embrace, truth unfurls,
A timeless bond in a world of pearls.

Frosted Ink on a Hidden Path

Upon the path where shadows creep,
The frost-kissed ink begins to seep.
Each step a whisper, soft and light,
In hidden realms, cloaked from sight.

The trees stand tall, their branches bare,
With secrets caught in frigid air.
A parchment scroll, the ground below,
Writes tales of ventures lost in snow.

Through swirling mists, lost voices call,
Inviting dreams to rise and fall.
Unraveled tales on icy scripts,
Where every heart decides and grips.

With every turn, the world unfolds,
In frozen colors, stories told.
A spellbound journey waits to start,
Frosted ink ignites the heart.

So take a step, embrace the night,
Let magic guide your frozen flight.
For on this path, where few have tread,
Frosted ink leads, our hearts are fed.

The Ancient Gryphon and the Snowy Veil

In the realm where winters wane,
An ancient gryphon breaks the chain.
With wings of gold and eyes so bright,
It guards the secrets lost to night.

Through snowy veils, its spirit soars,
Among the whispers of ancient chores.
A guardian of the realms unseen,
In frozen dreams, it reigns serene.

Beneath the stars, the shadows play,
As night drapes softly, night meets day.
The gryphon calls, its voice a song,
A timeless echo, sharp and strong.

And in its flight, the cool winds sigh,
Through crystal air, the legends fly.
It weaves through realms where magic dwells,
In tales of old, where silence tells.

So fear not the snow's chilly breath,
For in its fold lies untold depth.
With each wingbeat, we rise and feel,
The ancient gryphon's snowy veil.

Dusk's Symphony in the Winged Grove

As dusk descends with colors bright,
A symphony plays in fading light.
The trees sway gently, whispers near,
In the winged grove, enchantments clear.

The owls take flight, their wisdom known,
In twilight's grasp, the magic grown.
Each rustling leaf, a note, a tune,
Beneath the watchful, silver moon.

The fireflies dance in glowing trails,
Each flicker spins a woven tale.
The nightingale, with voice so sweet,
Sings lullabies on twilight's beat.

With shadows soft, the world embraces,
Each note a brush on hidden faces.
In winged refrain, the night unfolds,
As dusk's symphony gently holds.

So linger long in this twilight art,
Let melodies awaken the heart.
For in the grove, where shadows play,
Dusk's symphony will guide your way.

Illusions of Light in the Frozen Woods

In frozen woods where shadows beam,
The light forms whispers, woven dream.
Through glistening frosts, illusions fight,
To dance the day into the night.

Where every bough is etched in glass,
The moonlight weaves through every mass.
In silence, secrets start to bloom,
A tapestry spun in nature's loom.

The crisp air crackles with delight,
As visions sway in flecks of light.
Ghostly shapes of old soften the chill,
With every flicker, hearts are still.

Amongst the pines, the echoes ring,
Of ancient songs that twilight brings.
In this frozen realm where shadows glide,
Illusions of light, our spirits ride.

So wander here, let warmth ignite,
The spark of wonder in the night.
For in these woods where tales entwine,
Illusions of light, forever shine.

Whispers of the Shadowed Drift

In twilight's grip, the shadows weave,
A tale of night that none believe.
The trees stand tall, their secrets deep,
As whispers dance where silence sleeps.

The moonlight spills on silver streams,
Where stars ignite forgotten dreams.
With every breath, the dark unfolds,
A magic spun in threads of gold.

A fleeting glance, a shape that fades,
In darkened woods, where joy invades.
Each rustling leaf, a silent call,
The shadows drift, embracing all.

Through tangled paths, through misty air,
Adventure lies in every stare.
With hearts alight, we start to roam,
In whispered woods, we find our home.

The Frosted Whisper of Myth

Upon the hill, the frost does gleam,
A land where whispers weave a dream.
The chill of night, a soft embrace,
Where legends twine with starlit grace.

The ancient tales of yore arise,
Beneath the cold, the magic lies.
Each step we take on covered ground,
Unraveling dreams, in silence found.

With every breath, the stories swell,
Within the frost, they weave their spell.
A mirthful laugh, a distant cheer,
In echos past, those we hold dear.

The moonlit glow, a silver guide,
We tread the path, where spirits bide.
In frozen hush, our quest begins,
As wonder sparkles, and warmth within.

Echoes in the Snow-Blanketed Glen

In the glen where shadows play,
Echoes linger, soft and gray.
The snowflakes fall, a quilted shroud,
Where whispers form, both bright and loud.

The trees hold secrets in their boughs,
While winter's breath the stillness vows.
Each footfall silent, every glance,
Invites us deeper, to the dance.

The sparkle of the night unfolds,
As tales of magic, soft and bold.
In frozen realms, our spirits soar,
A world of wonder, evermore.

With hearts aglow, we gather near,
To share the warmth that conquers fear.
In snow-blanketed dreams we feel,
The echoes of what time may heal.

Secret Traces on a Moonlit Path

By moonlit paths, we wander slow,
Where secret traces hide below.
A gentle breeze whispers our fate,
In magic's arms, we contemplate.

The stars above, like diamonds shine,
In whispered tales, our hearts entwine.
Each step we take, a story shared,
In hushed tones, a world prepared.

The night reveals what daylight hides,
As ancient wisdom gently guides.
With every breath, our spirits rise,
Exploring depths beyond the skies.

Through shadows cast and moonlit beams,
We seek the truth within our dreams.
In every turn, a glimpse of light,
As secret traces hold us tight.

Whimsy of the Feathered Watcher

Upon the branches, shadows play,
The feathered watcher keenly stays.
With twinkling eyes, they peek and call,
In whispered winds, they hear it all.

Through golden leaves, they flit and chase,
A dance of joy in nature's grace.
With every chirp, a secret shared,
In vibrant rhythms, hearts are bared.

As dusk descends, the world transforms,
The feathers rustle, the night adorns.
In dreams of flight, they take their stand,
Where magic sings across the land.

Each flutter tells of tales long gone,
Of ancient woods where shadows yawn.
In harmony with stars above,
The feathered watcher whispers love.

Echoing Frost upon the Forgotten Trails

Upon the paths where memories lie,
Echoes of frost under a pale sky.
The silence swirls like a gentle sigh,
Where whispers of old dreams softly die.

Each step we take on this frozen ground,
Hints of a past in silence found.
The biting chill holds stories tight,
Of laughter lost, of fleeting light.

In twilight's glow, shadows creep,
While drifts of snow in slumber deep.
The trees stand guard, their branches bare,
A secret pact, a solemn prayer.

Through whispered winds, the tales are spun,
Of battles fought and battles won.
And in the quiet, the truth unfolds,
Of winter's touch on hearts so bold.

The Quiet Dance of Myth and Frost

In twilight's embrace, the legends twine,
A tapestry wrought with magic divine.
The dance of shadows, a silent ball,
Where frost-kissed dreams begin to call.

Through the emerald woods, whispers glide,
In misty realms where spirits bide.
Each breath of air carries tales untold,
In the quiet dance, the night grows bold.

A flicker of starlight on silver streams,
Sways to the rhythm of ancient dreams.
With each soft step, a promise made,
In the hush of night, fears begin to fade.

Where myth and frost caress the land,
In silence deep, we understand.
The world awakens, its wonders bright,
In the quiet dance of the starry night.

Chimerical Dreams Beneath the Winter's Veil

Beneath the quilt of winter's white,
Chimerical dreams take wondrous flight.
With swirling snowflakes, visions spin,
A landscape where the magic begins.

In every flake, a story lies,
Of distant shores and whispered skies.
The frost-kissed air carries sweet delight,
As dreams are woven in the night.

Where laughter dances on icy streams,
And hope is wrapped in silvery dreams.
In the heart of winter's tender grace,
We find a warmth, a sacred place.

The stars above, like lanterns glow,
Guiding us through the chilling snow.
In chimerical realms where wishes sail,
We find our truth beneath winter's veil.

Guardians of the Winter's Heart

In the glades where frost does creep,
The guardians of winter vigil keep.
Whispers of magic fill the air,
With secrets that dance in the icy glare.

Each flake a story, soft and white,
Wrapped in silence, the dead of night.
They watch the stars with ancient eyes,
Guardians of truth 'neath winter skies.

With each breath, the chill does sing,
A melody forged from winter's wing.
They cradle dreams in their frosty grasp,
In stillness, life's moments entwined and clasped.

Through evergreen arches draped with snow,
The guardians whisper, their love aglow.
Amidst the cold, a warmth takes flight,
In the heart of winter, pure and bright.

As dawn creeps in, with hues so rare,
The guardians fade, yet linger there.
For in the chill, their spirits stay,
In every heartbeat, come what may.

Eternal Silence in the Feathered Domain

Beneath the branches, shadows play,
In feathered realms where silence lay.
A hush descends, soft as a sigh,
As twilight wraps the earth, nearby.

Birds of winter sit in rows,
With secrets only the silence knows.
Their feathers glint in moonlit beams,
The night alive with whispered dreams.

Eternal peace in the cool night air,
A world suspended, free from care.
Echoes of wings, like gentle lace,
In this quiet, a sacred space.

The stars like lanterns, bright and clear,
Guide the way for those who hear.
The softest rustle, a call to roam,
In this silent realm, we've found our home.

Wrapped in night, we wander free,
In harmony with the melody.
A feathered domain of still delight,
Where silence reigns, and hearts take flight.

The Luminous Path Through Winter's Bower

In winter's bower, a path unfolds,
Luminous glitter, a tale retold.
Each step a spark in the cold, crisp air,
Guides the way with a gentle care.

Trees draped in lace, silver and white,
Stand as sentinels through the night.
A lantern's glow, soft and warm,
Leads the wanderer safe from harm.

The whispers of frost on branches sway,
As starlight dances, bright as day.
In this enchanted, snowy scene,
Magic weaves a thread unseen.

With every footfall, the heart does sing,
Embraced by winter's wondrous wings.
A tapestry spun from dreams and light,
In the bower's glow, all souls take flight.

Beyond the path, where shadows blend,
A promise dwells, where journeys end.
Through winter's bower, a truth so rare,
A luminous love forever there.

Echoes of Shadows Beneath the Snowy Sky

In the realm where silence dwells,
Echoes of shadows weave their spells.
Beneath the cold, a story waits,
Unlocking dreams at winter's gates.

Footsteps muffled by a blanket white,
Echo gently fades into night.
The world transformed, untouched, anew,
Under the gaze of the silvered view.

Whispers of trees, their secrets glow,
Beneath the heavy, drifting snow.
A silent pact with the darkened earth,
In every flake, a herald of rebirth.

Each shadow dances, soft and low,
To a rhythm only the moon can know.
In this stillness, the heart beats slow,
Tracing the echoes, where stories grow.

A tapestry woven with silver thread,
Of whispers, shadows, and words unsaid.
Beneath the sky, forever drawn,
Echoes of winter greet the dawn.

Whispers of Dark Winter's Embrace

In the silence of the night, cold winds sigh,
Whispers linger as shadows pass by.
Beneath a cloak of snow, secrets lie,
Dark winter's embrace, where dreams go to die.

Trees stand bare, with branches like bones,
Echoes of laughter turn to soft moans.
Frost weaves its lace on forgotten stones,
A tapestry spun where the heartache groans.

From ancient paths where the lost wander,
Footsteps muffled, as thoughts start to ponder.
The stars above in their distant wonder,
Guard all the souls that winter has laundered.

Crimson hues bleed into twilight's mist,
Silhouettes dance as if they can't resist.
Hope floats gently, like a lover's tryst,
In dark winter's arms, stillness is kissed.

Yet spring's promise lies under the frost,
A flame of warmth, though at times we're lost.
Through shadows deep, we'll pay any cost,
For in winter's depths, true magic is tossed.

Shadows Dance on Frosted Ground

Under the moonlight, shadows take flight,
A ballet of secrets, all cloaked in the night.
Frosted whispers, where fantasies ignite,
Dancing with echoes, in ghostly delight.

Crisp air envelops with a shiver's embrace,
As dreams pirouette in this desolate place.
With every footfall, time slows its pace,
In the frost-bitten nooks, we find our grace.

Beneath a canopy of glistening white,
Moonbeams shimmer, roads gleam bright.
The heart stirs slowly, drawn to the light,
While shadows dance softly, banishing fright.

An orchestra plays in currents of chill,
Notes wrapped in silence, all time seems to still.
Each whisper of winter, a potent thrill,
Invites us to dream with a fervent will.

Yet as dawn creeps, shadows draw near,
Frosted ground warms, while the edges clear.
In the light of day, we surrender our fear,
To shadows that danced, now gentle, sincere.

The Silent Vale of Midnight Feathers

In the vale where midnight softly weeps,
Feathers drift lightly, where slumber keeps.
Stars cradle wishes, as silence creeps,
Into the hearts of those lost in deep sleeps.

Whispers of dreams on the edge of the night,
Glimmers of wonder, of hope taking flight.
In shadows entwined, the moon shines bright,
Guardians of secrets in timeless twilight.

Along the banks of a still, icy stream,
Midnight feathers float on a silver beam.
Each gentle touch conjures a delicate dream,
Where the essence of night feels more like a theme.

The world wrapped in silver, soft as a sigh,
Where worries dissolve and sweet illusions fly.
In this silent vale, no goodbyes, no lie,
Just echoes of love that linger nearby.

When dawn emerges, a tender embrace,
Feathers ascend in the softening space.
Yet the silent vale will always keep trace,
Of midnight's whispers in its hidden grace.

Celestial Ink in a Winter's Dream

Beneath a canopy of shimmering stars,
Cold winds carry tales from afar.
Celestial ink trails in the night,
Painting the world in ethereal light.

Snowflakes whisper secrets of ages old,
Stories embroidered in silver and gold.
Through stillness, new memories are told,
As winter wraps night in its blanket bold.

In this dreamscape, reality blurs,
As visions arise and enchantment stirs.
Glistening crystals like fine embroidery spurred,
Crafting a world through the heart's soft purrs.

The night breathes magic, wrapped in a sigh,
Where wishes take flight, learning to fly.
Beneath winter's gaze, our spirits draw nigh,
In celestial ink, there's no reason to cry.

When dawn's early blush breaks the frost's tight weave,
Dreams linger sweetly, for those who believe.
In the coldest of nights, we learn to retrieve,
The warmth of our hearts, and the magic we weave.

The Specters of the Silver-Cloaked Woods

Deep in the woods where the shadows dwell,
Silver cloaks shimmer, casting a spell.
Whispers of secrets, lost in the night,
Echoes of laughter, fading from sight.

Ghostly apparitions glide through the trees,
Dancing with moonlight, swaying with ease.
Their essence lingers, soft as a sigh,
As twilight embraces the stars up high.

Branches entwined, like fingers of fate,
Guarding the stories, both tender and great.
The specters await with tales to be told,
Of love and of loss, of dreams turned to gold.

A flicker of hope in the night's gentle fold,
Where memories glisten like silver and gold.
To wander these woods is to open one's heart,
To dance with the specters, never to part.

So heed the allure of the silver-cloaked blight,
Where shadows and moonbeams entwine in the night.
For those brave enough to step through the veil,
Will find the true magic where mortals must pale.

When Shadows Meet the Snowy Glade

When shadows meet in the snowy glade,
A hush blankets all, a delicate shade.
Footprints of whispers laid out in white,
Tracing the secrets of day into night.

Beneath the still branches, the world seems to freeze,
Awakening magic, the heart's gentle tease.
Snowflakes like stars fall in soft, radiant spins,
Dancing with joy, where the dreamer begins.

The glade holds a promise, a world yet unknown,
Where laughter and wonder can easily grow.
Shadows entwine with the shimmer of frost,
In a moment so fleeting, yet never quite lost.

So step with intention, let silence be sought,
For magic runs deep in this realm of pure thought.
Embrace every flurry, each whisper and thrill,
In the shadows that beckon, our hearts they will fill.

When shadows meet as the twilight does fade,
In the snowy glade, where memories are made.
Hold tight to the moment, let it weave in your soul,
For here lies the essence that makes a heart whole.

The Resplendent Mysteries of the Snowy Realm

In the snowy realm, where time softly glows,
Mysteries linger beneath icy snows.
Frosted whispers tell tales of the past,
Of shadows and stories that forever last.

Glittering crystals dance on winter's breath,
A canvas of dreams that defy even death.
Each twinkle a promise, each flake a new chance,
To lose oneself fully in winter's own dance.

Beneath the pale moon, where wishes take flight,
Resplendent enigmas beckon the night.
With every deep breath, the air shimmers bright,
In a world filled with wonders, awaiting our sight.

The soft crunch of snow beneath footsteps bold,
Leads us through corridors of white and of gold.
Here, magic awakens where silence unfolds,
And stories forgotten find space to be told.

So venture with courage into this expanse,
Find joy in the mysteries that beckon with chance.
For in the snowy realm, we'll uncover our dreams,
Adventuring onward, or so it seems.

Whirlwinds of Ink in Winter's Realm

In winter's realm, where silence sustains,
Whirlwinds of ink draw love's tender chains.
Fingers of frost trace the stories of old,
While hearts beat in rhythm, so fervent and bold.

The pages of time flutter soft in the breeze,
As memories scatter like leaves from the trees.
Each word holds a spell, a phantom embrace,
A world crafted gently, time cannot erase.

Ink flows like rivers, deep and profound,
Capturing moments where joy can be found.
The whispers of winter weave tales evermore,
Of love and adventure from shore unto shore.

Beneath starry skies, the ink takes its flight,
A symphony woven of shadow and light.
In every soft snowfall, a story takes form,
While whirlwinds of ink keep the heart ever warm.

So gather your thoughts in this winter's embrace,
As the realm calls to you, a sacred workspace.
Let the ink flow freely, let your spirit ascend,
For winter's true magic is found in a friend.

Echoes of the Eternal Winter Night

In icy halls where whispers dwell,
The moonlight weaves a silver spell.
Every shadow holds a tale,
Of frosted lands where silence wail.

Beneath the stars that shimmer bright,
Echoes dance in velvet night.
The frozen breeze, a gentle sigh,
Carries secrets from the sky.

The trees, adorned with crystal crowns,
Stand tall against the world's frowns.
Each flake that falls, a wish in flight,
Lost within the eternal night.

As dreams entwine with winter's breath,
Time stands still, defying death.
In this realm where cold winds sing,
Life and magic brightly cling.

Thus we wander through the frost,
Seeking warmth, though we are lost.
In echoes of the night so deep,
Guarded dreams we dare to keep.

The Spellbound Glimmer of Dusk's Embrace

As day surrenders to twilight's kiss,
A whisper lingers, wrapped in bliss.
Colors blend, a wondrous art,
Painting dreams upon the heart.

The sky ignites in amber glow,
Where magic flows in rivers slow.
Each star awakens, one by one,
A symphony of night begun.

In shadows cast by setting sun,
The spellbound glimmer of life begun.
Creatures stir in twilight's grace,
In silence, they find their place.

Moonbeams weave through branches wide,
With secrets shared, they softly glide.
The world in hues of dusky charms,
Cradles all in nature's arms.

So let us dance 'neath velvet skies,
Where wonders spark and hope replies.
In dusk's embrace, we find our way,
As night unfolds a bright ballet.

A Tapestry of Stars and Shadows

In the heart of night, shadows play,
Weaving dreams in a grand display.
Stars twinkle with a guiding light,
Leading us through the depths of night.

A tapestry spun with silver thread,
Shows the journey of dreams we've led.
Whispers soar on the midnight breeze,
A symphony of heart's unease.

With every pulse, the shadows dance,
In the rhythm of a dreamer's trance.
Each flicker holds a story told,
A glimpse of magic, bright and bold.

Through the cosmos, we drift and glide,
In this wonder, we shall abide.
For in the dark, we find our way,
Amongst the stars that choose to stay.

Thus we wander, shadows in tow,
In the vastness where dreams freely flow.
In the tapestry of night so grand,
Together we weave, hand in hand.

Frostbitten Dreams in the Realm of Beasts

In misty woods where shadows roam,
Frostbitten dreams find their home.
The whispering winds tell tales of old,
Of beasts and magic, fierce and bold.

Moonlight dances on frozen ground,
In the silence, secrets abound.
Each creature stirs from restless sleep,
Guarding promises we must keep.

Snowflakes drift like timeless sighs,
In the realm where wonder lies.
Beasts awaken, fierce yet gentle,
In the glow of dreams, they are sentimental.

Together they tread through midnight's breath,
In the stillness that softens death.
A bond unbroken, wild and free,
In this frostbitten tapestry.

So let the night's magic unfurl,
In the realm where dreams gently swirl.
For in the heart of the beast, we find,
A reflection of our own kind.

Chronicles of the Frosted Animals

In the whispering woods of silver and white,
Frosted creatures dance in the pale moonlight.
Snowflakes twinkle like stars on a thread,
As tales of the winter are lovingly spread.

The hare leaps softly, a phantom of grace,
While owls silently glide, in the calm embrace.
Each paw print a story, each feather a song,
In this frosted realm where the brave all belong.

The fox in his coat of the brightest of flame,
Watches the night as he carries his name.
With eyes like two embers, he prowls through the chill,
A guardian of secrets, he follows his will.

Through thickets entwined with a crystalline veil,
All creatures converge, in a hushed, reverent tale.
The whispers of winter embrace every heart,
In the chronicles told, they will never depart.

So let the frost linger, let the world hold its breath,
In the silence of snow, there is beauty in death.
For each life must fade, yet in tales they will soar,
Forever enchanted, forever adored.

The Dance of Shadows on the Frostbitten Ground

Underneath the moon where shadows entwine,
The frostbitten ground feels the weight of time.
Figures emerge through a veil of the night,
Dancing with secrets, absorbing the light.

With a flicker and sway, the shadows come alive,
As winter spirits whisper, and cold breezes thrive.
They twist and they turn, in a mystical trance,
Inviting the stars to join in the dance.

Buffeted by winds that carry the chill,
The shadows spin forth with an ethereal thrill.
Each leap they take is a story unspooled,
In a world cloaked in magic, where silence is ruled.

Glistening frost reminds us of the past,
Of fleeting moments and spells that were cast.
Yet here in the now, we watch and reflect,
As the dance of the shadows does softly connect.

So linger awhile where the frost kisses ground,
And learn from the grace of the shadows around.
For in their embrace, we discover the art,
Of finding our place in the world, and the heart.

The Veiled Secrets of Celestial Beasts

In the still of the night where the stars softly gleam,
Celestial beasts stir in a dream within dreams.
They weave through the clouds, with a mystical grace,
Guardians of wonders, in a hidden space.

A stag with fine antlers of shimmering light,
Carries old wisdom, far out of sight.
While a silver-winged bird sings a song of the skies,
Revealing the truths that no mortal eye spies.

With whispers of magic that tingle the air,
These creatures of legend, beyond time, beyond care.
They dance with the cosmos, in shadows and glow,
An ancient connection, too deep to know.

They ride on the winds where the dreams intertwine,
Speaking in verses of ages divine.
Each moment a gift, wrapped in starlight and lore,
Eternally seeking what lies at the core.

So listen, dear friend, to the hush of the night,
For the veiled secrets dwell in the softest of light.
In the depths of the cosmos, a truth we may find,
As the celestial beasts guide our hearts and our minds.

Velvet Nightfall in a Snowbound World

When velvet night drapes its soft, gentle hue,
And the world wraps its arms in a blanket of blue,
The snowbound terrain is a canvas so bright,
Where dreams come alive in the hush of the night.

Crystal stars shimmer like gems in the sky,
As winter's embrace whispers soft lullabies.
Each flake is a wish, each drift a delight,
In this silent expanse, where all feels just right.

The trees wear their crystals with shimmering pride,
Guardians of secrets where silence can bide.
In the heart of the stillness, a promise unfurls,
Against the backdrop of snowflakes and swirls.

As the moon casts a glow on the quietest ground,
Hope dances together with peace all around.
In the velvet nightfall, we find our own peace,
And the worries of day slowly start to cease.

So let us embrace this enchanted retreat,
Where magic and wonder join hands at our feet.
In this snowbound world, full of beauty and grace,
We discover our dreams in this soft, sacred space.

The Ethereal Whispers of Winter Legends

In the hush of the frosty night,
Legends shimmer, pale and bright.
Snowflakes dance, a silent song,
Winter's magic, where dreams belong.

Moonlight bathes the sleeping trees,
Winds carry tales upon the freeze.
Whispers weave through the chilly air,
Echoes of stories, ancient and rare.

Beneath the stars, a glow unfolds,
Carving secrets in frosty molds.
Frozen rivers, a path unclear,
Guide the brave hearts, ever near.

With every breath, the chill will tell,
Of heroes lost in a winter spell.
Voices linger, sweet and low,
In ethereal realms where wonders grow.

So listen close when the night is still,
Embrace the whispers that time can't kill.
For in the heart of icy land,
The legends of winter forever stand.

The Frosted Horizon and the Winged Silence

Above the frost-kissed peaks so high,
Wings unfurl, beneath the gray sky.
Silent flights in the shimmering dawn,
Echo the tales that the ancients draw.

A blanket of snow spreads wide and bright,
Glistening softly in the silver light.
The world breathes deep, in calm repose,
Finding solace where the cold wind blows.

Mountains whisper to the stars above,
In the quietude, a sea of love.
Every flake holds a secret long told,
In the stillness, memories unfold.

Through icy realms, the winged ones soar,
Guardians of tales from ancient lore.
They carry the dreams of those below,
On currents of air, in the silent glow.

As twilight descends and shadows creep,
In the winter's heart, the world falls asleep.
With each whisper of wings in the night,
The frosted horizon sparkles with light.

Chronicles Beneath the Icy Canopy

Beneath the boughs where the frost does cling,
Chronicles hidden await the spring.
Icicles shimmer like slivers of dreams,
Life sleeps softly under snow's gentle seams.

Whispers of stories lie drifted and still,
In the shadowed glades where time bends to chill.
Each crystal petal and frigid breath,
Holds echoing laughter, and whispers of death.

Through the hushed woods, the echoes remain,
Of joyous feasts and heart-wrenching pain.
The trees hold secrets, old as the stars,
Etched in the bark, like timeless memoirs.

As the world whispers through branches and boughs,
The chronicles beckon with solemn vows.
While winter prevails, in a blanket of white,
The heart of the forest keeps stories tight.

So move through the frost with a wonderer's heart,
For places of magic are seldom apart.
Beneath the icy canopy's hold,
Are chronicles whispered in silence, retold.

Shadows of the Celestial Portents

In the twilight's grasp, shadows twist and weave,
Celestial portents, what webs they conceive.
Stars shimmer softly, like eyes in the night,
Whispering omens on wings of twilight.

The moon casts a glow, gentle and rare,
Illuminating secrets concealed in the air.
In every flicker, a truth takes flight,
Guiding lost souls through the deepest of night.

With every breath, the cosmos sighs,
In the tapestry woven, the past never dies.
Eclipsed by fate, the whispers reveal,
The forces unseen that stars will conceal.

As shadows arise from the depths of the dark,
Holding patterns of fate, they spark.
Glimmers of futures unfold beneath glass,
In twilight's embrace, where moments shall pass.

So heed these shadows, this celestial dance,
For woven in night is a spirited chance.
The portents of destiny glint in your eye,
In the silent, star-studded, eternal sky.

Shadows of the Celestial Beast

In night's embrace, a whisper calls,
The stars alight where silence falls.
A creature stirs in hidden grace,
With gleaming eyes, it claims its space.

It weaves through shadows, soft and sly,
A guardian of the midnight sky.
With wings spread wide, it stirs the breeze,
A moonlit dance among the trees.

Each heartbeat echoes, deep and low,
Beneath the glow of silver snow.
The beast of lore, with power vast,
In solitude, it sweeps the past.

Its presence chills, yet ignites awe,
A spectral form, a fleeting flaw.
In every flash, it leaves a mark,
A fleeting ghost, a glint, a spark.

So whisper soft the tales of night,
For in the dark, there's hidden light.
The celestial beast, forever free,
A shadowed dream for you and me.

Ethereal Frost in the Woodland Realm

In woodlands deep, where silence reigns,
The frost awakens, soft refrains.
Each crystal flake, a story spun,
A dance of glimmers 'neath the sun.

The branches bow with icy grace,
A tapestry, a crystal lace.
Each breath is visible, pure and bright,
The world adorned in winter's light.

The whispers there are soft and low,
Where ethereal wonders start to grow.
With every step, the echoes sing,
Of timeless tales the seasons bring.

Among the trees, a hush does spread,
Where nature sleeps, and dreams are bred.
In shimmering calm, the heart finds peace,
As time stands still, and worries cease.

So wander deep in frost's embrace,
In woodland realms, find your place.
For in the chill, the warmth does dwell,
A magic spun, a tranquil spell.

The Lament of the Winter-Winged Guardian

Upon the peak where silence lingers,
A guardian weeps with frozen fingers.
With feathers white as purest snow,
It mourns for dreams that cease to flow.

In twilight hours, when shadows creep,
Its sorrow sings, a lullaby deep.
For every loss, a tear does fall,
In echoes that haunt the midnight call.

Through tempest winds, its spirit fights,
To guard the world through long, cold nights.
Yet still it grieves for light once known,
A lonely path, forever flown.

Among the stars, it seeks the past,
In fleeting glimmers, memories cast.
The guardian's heart, a well of ache,
In winter's grasp, it bends, it breaks.

Yet hope prevails in darkest hour,
The strength of love becomes its power.
So with each dawn's embrace of light,
The guardian rises, ready to fight.

Veils of Ink and Crystal Dreams

In night's embrace, where shadows blend,
A tapestry of whispers wend.
With veils of ink, and crystals bright,
A world unfolds beyond our sight.

Each dream is woven with gentle care,
In cosmic threads that dance in air.
The stories of old come forth to play,
In celestial hues, they drift away.

The stars align in graceful arcs,
While secrets hum in twilight sparks.
Each thought a note, each gaze a beam,
In this realm of ink and crystal dream.

The moonlight spills like liquid grace,
As shadows lend their soft embrace.
A symphony of night unfolds,
A tale of wonders to be told.

So let your heart roam wild and free,
In veils where fantasy longs to be.
For in the depths of dream's grand scheme,
Awaits the light behind the gleam.

Beneath the Starlit Canopy

Whispers weave through the night air,
Soft glimmers hug the tree's heart,
Dreams dance on silvery threads,
In shadows where magic can start.

Moonlight spills like liquid glass,
On secrets held within the glade,
With starlight woven in their grasp,
Those silent tales never do fade.

Each breeze carries a ghostly song,
Of worlds unfurling like a tale,
Where wonder blooms, and time is wrong,
As night's embrace begins to sail.

Underneath the voiceless skies,
A realm exists both strange and wide,
With laughter caught in midnight sighs,
In dreams where all the shadows hide.

Beneath the starlit canopy,
The heart of magic softly beats,
In echoes lost, we're finally free,
Where time and space entwine like sweets.

The Inked Silence of Enchanted Wilds

In whispers deep where shadows play,
The ink of night begins to write,
Stories born from dusk till day,
In wilds where magic stirs in sight.

With every rustle, secrets bloom,
As twilight paints a mystic shade,
Beneath the stars, a quiet room,
Where ancient wonders are displayed.

Leaves flutter like pages turned,
Each breath a tale of heart and fate,
Through twisted trunks, the lanterns burned,
Luring souls who learn to wait.

Silence wraps like velvet night,
A tapestry of peace and dread,
In echoing whispers, tales ignite,
Daunting paths where others tread.

Entwined in dreams that nature shares,
We wander deep through inked designs,
With every step, the wild declares,
A world where magic intertwines.

A Canvas of Frost-Kissed Legends

A hush descends on winter's breath,
As frost paints stories on the air,
Each crystal shimmers, hinting death,
Yet life beneath is hidden there.

Legends whisper through the pines,
In every flake, a tale reposed,
Where silence breeds the coldest signs,
And nature's heart is deftly closed.

Thrones of ice and crowns of white,
Embrace the dreams from days of yore,
In glimmers that hold onto light,
A canvas stretched across the floor.

In reverent hush, the world does pause,
A delicate quilt where whispers blend,
To weave the magic from the stars,
And in the stillness, time must mend.

Awash in glints of moonbeam's glow,
We find the legends wrapped in frost,
Through winter's dance, we're free to know,
All that is gained, and nothing lost.

Celestial Patterns in the Wintry Embrace

In winter's grasp, the cosmos gleams,
As starlight weaves its gentle care,
In shadows, whispering secret dreams,
With patterns spun in chilled, crisp air.

Each flake a wish from heaven sent,
Dancing softly through the night,
To mark a tale of wonderment,
As constellations glow with light.

Beneath the quilt of twilight's grace,
The earth and sky begin to blend,
In every corner of this space,
A truth unfolds where hearts can mend.

The icy breath holds spirits dear,
In silence where the echoes play,
A melody we long to hear,
As winter's heart shows us the way.

Celestial patterns weave and twine,
In every breath, a story traced,
In wintry realms, our souls align,
As dreams take flight in soft embrace.

The Frosty Cloak of Mystical Beings

In twilight glow, the shadows dance,
A frosty cloak, in moonlight's trance.
With whispers soft, they share their lore,
In secret glades, on ancient shore.

The silver mist wraps round their form,
In chill of night, where spirits swarm.
They weave through trees, in quiet glee,
As magic hums, wild and free.

Beware the frost that bites the skin,
For wonders lie where few have been.
A single touch, a fleeting glance,
Can cast the heart in timeless trance.

The cloaks they wear, of shimmering light,
Guard tales of old, and endless night.
Their laughter ringing through the cold,
In whispered words, the secrets told.

So tread with care beneath the stars,
Where time dissolves, and dreamers are.
For in the frost, the mysteries gleam,
In every step, the threads of dream.

Legends of the Frostbound Grove

In the frostbound grove where time stands still,
Legends stir with a silent thrill.
Whispers of giants, tall and grand,
A realm untouched by human hand.

Beneath the boughs, where shadows creep,
Old stories rise from ancient sleep.
The air is thick with magic's sigh,
As stars gaze down from the velvet sky.

With every step, the earth does hum,
In echoes soft, the past will come.
Through icy winds, in whispers low,
The essence of ages starts to flow.

Hear the calls of the creatures rare,
Buried in frost, hidden with care.
They guard the tales of love and loss,
Each path they tread, a sacred cross.

So wander forth where shadows blend,
In every corner, a tale to send.
For in the frost, the legends wake,
To guide the brave, their hearts to take.

The Glistening Veil of Forgotten Myths

Beneath the moon, a veil does gleam,
In twilight's grasp, the lost ones dream.
Forgotten myths of yesteryears,
Reveal their truths through ancient tears.

In every glimmer, a story brews,
Where magic reigns, and hope renews.
A tapestry woven with care and grace,
In glistening threads, the past we trace.

The stars above, in silence weep,
For dreams once sown in the dark they keep.
A flickering flame, a ghostly light,
Enfolds the night in pure delight.

With every whisper, the woods align,
In harmony, the fates entwine.
Each myth, a seed that bids to grow,
In hearts where love and courage flow.

So take the veil, and hold it tight,
Let stories guide you through the night.
For in the glistening, the past reveals,
The magic wrapped in time's soft peels.

Enigmas of the Enchanted Expanse

In the enchanted expanse where wonders dwell,
Enigmas twirl beneath the spell.
With every breeze, a secret calls,
Through winding paths and hidden walls.

The trees stand tall, with stories deep,
In shadows where the lost ones sleep.
They guard the truth with silent grace,
In every corner, a whispered trace.

The river sings of ages past,
Its waters whisper tales amassed.
Each ripple holds a thought from long ago,
In currents swift, the dreams still flow.

So wander forth with heart aflame,
In enchanted realms, find your name.
For in the enigmas, freedom lies,
In the expanse where every soul flies.

Embrace the magic, let it unfurl,
In the heartbeat of the world's great swirl.
For in every step, a sorcery lies,
In the enchanted expanse, where the spirit flies.

Sentinels of Shadows and White Silence

In the twilight where whispers weave,
Sentinels watch, their silence reprieve.
The frost-bitten air carries a sigh,
As shadows stretch beneath the grey sky.

Glimmers of light spark dreams anew,
While stars above spin tales askew.
Beneath their gaze, the world holds its breath,
In the calm embrace of timeless depth.

Each tree an altar, each stone a song,
Guarded secrets where souls belong.
Echoes of laughter float from the past,
As night unfolds her shadowy cast.

With every chill, the moment grows fraught,
For in the silence, true magic is wrought.
The sentinels stand with vigilant grace,
In the dance of shadows, they find their place.

Bound by the night, yet kissed by the dawn,
The saga of stillness quietly drawn.
A canvas of darkness and silver design,
In the realm of the unseen, where stars align.

Frozen Elegy of the Mystic Vale

Amidst the frost in the vale of dreams,
Nature whispers, and the starlight gleams.
A tapestry woven with threads of night,
Holds tales of wonder, both eerie and bright.

The trees stand still, like guardians wise,
Veiled in snow, under watchful skies.
Every flake a story, a memory kept,
In the heart of the vale, where the ancients slept.

Echoing softly, the echoes chime,
Each whispering wind speaks of forgotten time.
Ghosts of the past drift through the chill,
In the frozen elegy, they linger still.

The crystal air sparkles, a hush envelops,
As shadows gather and silence develops.
The moon casts a glow on the land so bare,
In the mystic vale, magic hangs in the air.

Awaken the spirits, let them take flight,
In this frozen embrace of enchanting night.
Where echoes and shadows forever entwine,
In the heart of the vale, lies the sacred shrine.

Portraits of Enchantment in Cold Twilight

In twilight's brush, the world takes shape,
Where echoes of wonder weave and drape.
Brushstrokes of silver upon the deep blue,
Frame portraits of magic, both old and new.

Frost-laden petals in a soft embrace,
Whisper stories of time and place.
Each moment captured with delicate grace,
In the gallery of dusk, where dreams interlace.

Stars twinkle like gems, in the canvas high,
As the moon spills secrets, a lullaby.
Each shadow a dancer, a tale to unfold,
In this portrait of enchantment, mysteries told.

The air hums softly with ancient lore,
A symphony played, forevermore.
In every heartbeat, the magic ignites,
Painting the darkness with luminous lights.

As twilight deepens, the world feels alive,
In this cold embrace, where wonders thrive.
Every breath taken is a brush with delight,
In the portraits of enchantment, all is made right.

The Dance of Omens in the Silent Snow

Beneath a veil of soft, silent snow,
Whispers of omens dance to and fro.
Each flake that falls carries tales untold,
In the quiet of winter, mysteries unfold.

The moonlight glistens on the fields aglow,
While shadows sway in a graceful flow.
A ballet of silence, each moment divine,
As nature entwines her secrets in line.

Birds take flight, responding to dreams,
In their fleeting paths, the starlight beams.
Glimmers of fortune in the paths they trace,
Every movement a sign in this sacred space.

With every breath, the stillness speaks,
A harmony woven that echoes for weeks.
The dance of omens in the frosty light,
Guiding lost souls through the cold, starry night.

So heed the signs as the seasons turn,
In the dance of the snow, deep lessons to learn.
For in every silence, magic takes flight,
In the heart of the winter, our spirits ignite.

The Guardians of the Darkened Crest

In shadows deep, the guardians dwell,
With secrets wrapped in a whispered spell.
They watch the night with a steadfast eye,
Bound by promises that never die.

Across the moors, their spirits glide,
A flicker of hope where the brave confide.
With every beat, a tale unfolds,
Of courage found and valor bold.

Through ancient woods, where the heartbeats echo,
Their presence felt in the light of the meadow.
Together they stand, unwavering and strong,
A family united where they belong.

As twilight falls and shadows merge,
In the silent pact, their destinies surge.
The guardians stand, a beacon so bright,
Illuminating the path through the night.

In the heart of the dark, where spirits soar,
Whispers of legends echo evermore.
For those who seek through the woeful quest,
Will find the strength of the darkened crest.

Emblems of Frost and Winged Light

In the morning chill, where the frost does gleam,
Emblems of winter weave a dream.
With wings of light that shimmer and sway,
They dance through the dawn of a new day.

Silver streams run beneath the snow,
As whispers of magic begin to flow.
Each feathered flake, a story in flight,
Crafting the tapestry of soft morning light.

From treetops high to valleys low,
They share their secrets in soft, gentle glow.
In the stillness found in the amber hue,
The world wakes anew, adorned with dew.

With every gust, they rise and twirl,
Graceful as dreams, in a magical whirl.
Emblems of frost, in their radiant dance,
Invite us to join in a silent romance.

As dusk draws near and shadows play,
Wonders of winter begin to sway.
Through the crisp air, a song takes flight,
Emblems of hope in the soft twilight.

The Serenade of Enchanted Snowflakes

They fall like whispers from hands of fate,
A serenade sweet, where dreams await.
With each delicate spin, a symphony grows,
Of laughter and joy, where magic flows.

Doctor winds carry their graceful play,
Over rooftops and paths where children sway.
Softly they settle, a blanket of white,
Kissing the earth in the still of night.

As shadows stretch and the twilight calls,
The snowflakes twirl, like sprightly thralls.
With artistry woven in patterns divine,
Each flake tells a tale, both yours and mine.

In a dance with the moon, they sparkle and gleam,
A tapestry woven from a shared dream.
The enchanted snowflakes, aglow in the light,
Carry our wishes through the winter's night.

So gather 'round under skies so vast,
Let laughter and love be forever steadfast.
In the serenade soft, where wonder takes flight,
Embrace the enchantment that glimmers so bright.

Echoes of Wingbeats in the Dusk

As day fades softly into the night,
The echoes of wingbeats take their flight.
Through whispers of twilight, a story is spun,
Of journeys begun, as the stars become one.

Shadows awaken with each gentle beat,
Memories linger, bittersweet.
The horizon blushes with colors untold,
A canvas alive, both vibrant and bold.

In the hush of dusk, where silence sings,
The dance of the night brings magical things.
With feathers of twilight, they glide and sway,
Guardians of secrets as night turns to day.

The heavens quiver under their grace,
A heart's wild rhythm in this timeless space.
As echoes resound in the velvet embrace,
Every beat holds a dream, each wing finds its place.

So listen closely to the songs of the night,
For echoes of wingbeats will lead you to light.
In the hush of the dusk, let your spirit soar free,
Embrace the magic that's whispered to thee.

www.ingramcontent.com/pod-product-compliance
Ingram Content Group UK Ltd.
Pitfield, Milton Keynes, MK11 3LW, UK
UKHW021420220125
4239UKWH00007B/168